ILLUSTRATED ENCYCLOPEDIA
NATURE

Managing Editor: Dr. Geeta Rani Arora
Editor: Ms. Pawanpreet Kaur
Education Consultant: Dr. Bimla Arora, *Shemrock School*
Copyright © with the publisher

Pegasus
An imprint of
B. Jain Publishers (P) Ltd.
USA - EUROPE - INDIA

NATURE

 ## Planet Earth

The earth is one of the eight planets of the solar system. The earth revolves around the sun in an elliptical orbit. The earth is the third planet from the sun and the fifth largest planet.

 ## Three Motions of the Earth

(1) Spins on its own axis.
(2) Travels around the sun.
(3) Moves through the Milky Way along with the rest of the solar system.

 ## Layers of the Earth

The earth is made up of four layers. The crust and mantle are the outermost layers, while the outer core and the inner core form the inner layers.

Quick Look

- Earth is the only planet in the universe known to have life.
- The solar system consists of the sun and eight planets.

As on April 2008, earth is home to 660,000,000 (6.66 billion) humans.

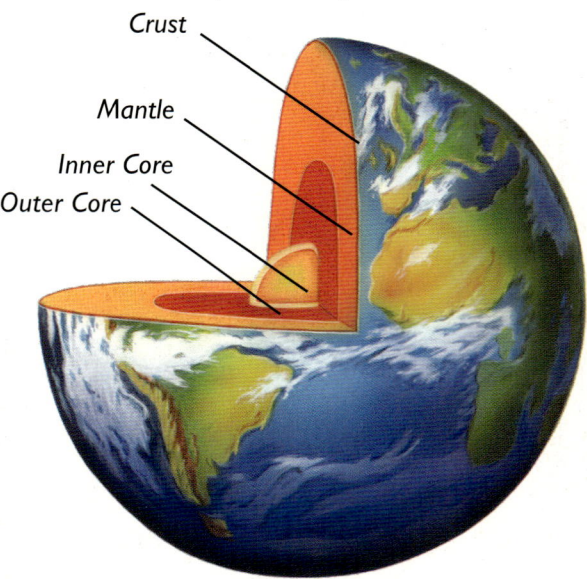

Layers of the earth.

Earth Fact File

Average Distance from the Earth to the Sun	:	149,669,180 km
Average Distance from the Earth to the Moon	:	384,403.1 km
Rotation on Axis	:	23 hours and 56 minutes and 04.09053 seconds
Revolution around Sun	:	365.2425 days
Circumference at the Equator	:	40,075.16 km
Circumference between the North and South Poles	:	40,008 km
Diameter at the Equator	:	12,756.1 km
Diameter at the Poles	:	12,713.5 km
Water Percentage	:	70.8%
Land Percentage	:	29.2%

THE EARTH

 Earth's Atmosphere Content

Nitrogen	:	78%
Oxygen	:	21%
Argon, carbon di-oxide and other gases	:	0.9%–0.03%

Layer	Average Depth (km)
Crust	21
Mantle	21–2,860
Outer core	2,860–5,100
Inner core	5,100–6,370

 Chemical Composition of the Earth

Iron	:	35%
Oxygen	:	29.5%
Silicon	:	15.2%
Magnesium	:	12.7%
Nickel	:	2.4%
Sulfur	:	1.9%
Titanium	:	0.05%

The atmosphere mostly contains nitrogen and oxygen.

 Highest, Lowest and Deepest

- Highest Elevation: Mt. Everest: 8,848 meters.
- Lowest Elevation on Land: Dead Sea: 420 meters below sea level.
- Deepest Point in the Ocean: Challenger Deep, Mariana Trench: 10,924 meters.

Satellite photograph of the Dead Sea.

Earth Temperature

Highest Temperature Recorded

Place	Date	Year	Temp
Al Aziziyah, Libya	September 13	1922	57.8°C

Lowest Temperature Recorded

Place	Date	Year	Temp
Vostok, Antarctica	July 21	1983	-89.2°C

NATURE

Quick Look

- Continents are large landmasses on the earth.
- Australia is the only country-continent on earth that has its own capital, Canberra.
- There area seven continents on earth.
- Africa is the second largest continent.

Asia

Area: 44,897,000 sq. km. (17,335,000 sq. mi.)

Population: 3,335,672,000

Main Languages: Chinese, Hindi, Bengali, Japanese, Punjabi, Javanese, Korean.

Main Religions: Hinduism, Islam, Buddhism, Christianity, Shintoism, Taoism, Zoroastrianism.

Largest Cities: Seoul, Mumbai, Jakarta, Tokyo, Shanghai.

Climate: Ranges from steaming hot temperatures to freezing cold mountains.

Asia is the largest continent.

Africa

Area: 30,319,000 sq. km. (11,706,000 sq. mi.)

Population: 656,108,000

Main Language Groups: Arabic, Hausa, Amharic, Yoruba, Oromo, Nguni, Igbo, Akan, Berber, and Malagasy.

Main Religions: Christianity, Islam, tribal religions, and Baha'i.

Largest Cities: Cairo, Egypt; Kinshasa, Zaire, and Alexandria, Egypt.

Climate: Very hot in deserts, tropical wet and dry, humid, subtropical, marine, warm temperate upland, and mountain.

CONTINENTS

South America

Area: 17,824,000 sq. km. (6,882,000 sq. mi.)

Population: more than 371,090,000 million

Main Languages: Spanish, Portuguese, and many Native American Languages.

Main Religions: Roman Catholicism, Protestantism, and others.

Largest Cities: Georgetown, Montevideo, Sucre, Lima, Valparaiso.

Climate: Every kind, most of the regions are tropical rainforest.

Europe

Area: 9,894,000 sq. km. (3,820,000 sq. mi.)

Population: 742,400,000

Main Languages: Russian, German, French, English, Italian, Ukrainian, Polish, Spanish, Romanian, Dutch, Serbo-Croatian.

Main Religions: Roman Catholicism, Eastern Orthodoxy, Protestantism, Judaism

Largest Cities: Moscow, London, Istanbul, St. Petersburg, Berlin.

Climate: Mostly temperate, average temperatures throughout the year and summers are cool and winters are mild.

Antarctica

Area: 14.4 million sq. km. (5.4 million sq. mi.)

Area is 12 percent of the earth.

Population: 0

Climate: Wind speed at most is 320 km/h.

Coldest temperature: -87°C

Warmest temperature: 15°C along the Antarctic Peninsula. Snowfall 5 cm in the middle and 51-101 cm on the coastlines.

Only two percent of Antarctica is ice-free.

Australia

Area: 7,682,292 sq. km. (2,966,133 sq. mi.)

Population: 18,508,000 (0.3% of world's population)

Main Language: English

Main Religions: Roman Catholicism, Protestantism, and Orthodox Christianity

Largest Cities: Sydney, Melbourne, Brisbane, Perth, Adelaide, Newcastle, and Canberra-Queanbeyan

Climate: 17–28°C in summers and 10–23°C in winters.

North America

Area: 24,709,000 sq. km. (9,540,000 sq. mi.)

Population: 529 million

Main Languages: English, French, Spanish

Main Religions: Roman Catholics, Protestants, Islam, Eastern Orthodoxy

Largest Cities: Mexico city, New York city, Los Angeles, Chicago, Santo Domingo, Havana, Guadalajara, Houston, Philadelphia, Nezahualcoyotle, San Diego, Monterrey, Detroit, Montreal, Pueblo, Dallas, Phoenix, San Antonio.

Climate: Arctic, sub arctic, tundra, marine, mountain, Mediterranean, temperate, highlands, interior plains, coastal plain, tropical, semiarid and arid.

NATURE

 ## What are cycles of nature?

Nature has various components within it such as water, nutrients (like nitrogen and oxygen) plants and animals. All the components interact with each other and with their non living environment to form an ecological unit. This interaction in the form of cycles renews the earth gradually.

 ## Water Cycle

The constant recycling of water within nature is called water cycle. The sunlight makes the water of oceans, rivers and lakes to evaporate and form water vapour. The water vapour rises up into the air and cools and condenses to form water droplets. Millions of water droplets form clouds and when they become heavy, rain or snow occurs. The rainwater falls into rivers and streams and flows back to oceans, seas and lakes to begin the water cycle again.

 ## Energy Cycle

Sun is the source of energy on earth. Sunlight and heat provides us energy for life. It is also used up by plants to make food and store energy. Animals cannot produce their own energy so they eat plants to get energy. When the plants and animals die, they release waste to the environment and heat of the sun is released back into the environment.

 ## Animal Life Cycle

A progression through a series of differing stages of development from which an organism passes is called life cycle. All animals have their unique way of reproduction and life cycle. Most animals lay eggs and only few give birth to live young ones. Insects, spiders, birds, amphibians and reptiles lay eggs while mammals give birth to live young ones.

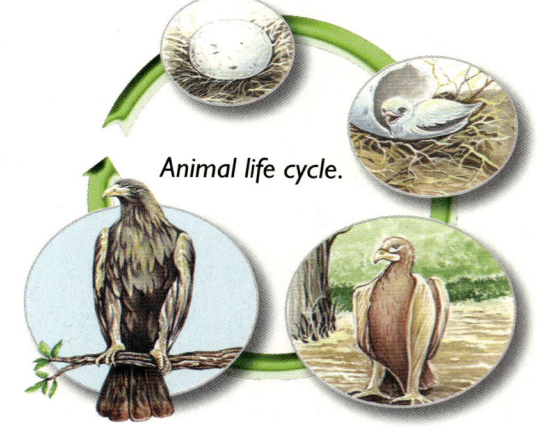

Animal life cycle.

NATURE'S CYCLES

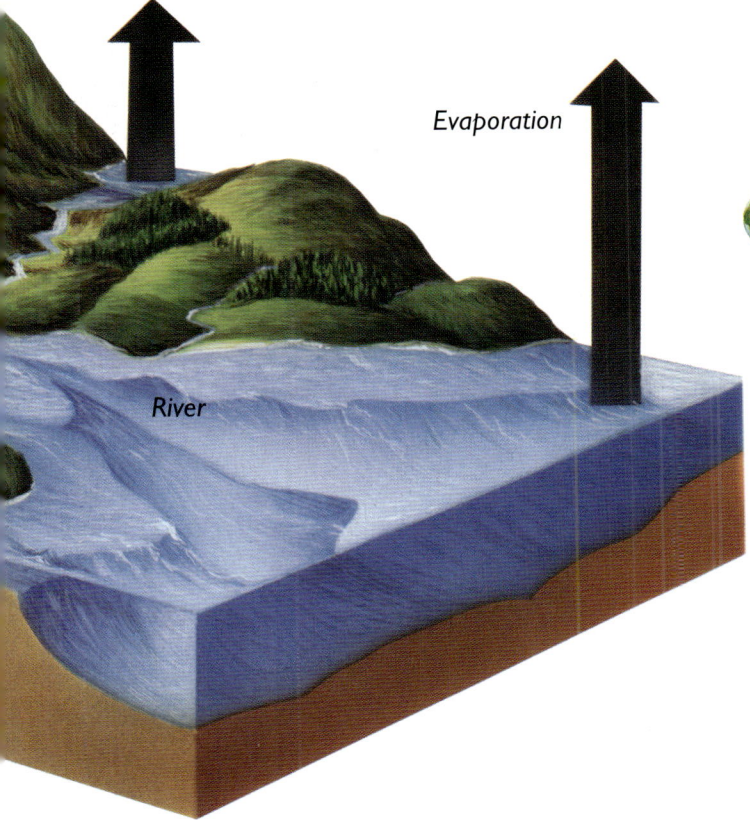

The earth's water cycle.

Carbon Cycle

Plants use carbon di-oxide for photosynthesis and make carbohydrates. Animals eat plants and take in these carbohydrates and use them for energy. When they breathe out carbon di-oxide into the air, it is again used by plants and thus the carbon cycle continues.

Nitrogen Cycle

The nitrogen found in the atmosphere, animal wastes and dead and decaying organisms is called the free nitrogen. But this can be used only by nitrogen-fixing bacteria that are found in soil. They convert the free nitrogen into usable forms that can be used by plants, which are further eaten by animals. The animal wastes and decaying plants and animals release the nitrogen again into the soil and thus the cycle continues.

Oxygen Cycle

In the process of photosynthesis, plants release oxygen into the atmosphere. We breathe in oxygen through respiration and release water and carbon di-oxide into the atmosphere. The plants absorb the carbon di-oxide and water to continue the cycle.

Quick Look

Water is everywhere on earth and covers 70% of the earth's surface.
There are 3.5 million species of animals worldwide ranging from the largest to the smallest.
Plants reproduce by seeds, spores, or cones.
Rock also goes through a cycle called rock cycle.
Carbon is found in all living organisms.
O_2 is the formula of oxygen and CO_2 is the chemical formula of carbon di-oxide.
97% of all the water on the earth is in the oceans so only 3% is fresh water.

NATURE

Climate

The word "climate" is derived from an ancient Greek word *kluimat*, which is commonly defined as the average weather of a place, typically over a period of around thirty years. The climate of a place is dependent on temperature, precipitation, wind, latitude, altitude and distance from the sea.

Climatic Types

Tropical climate	Oceanic climate
Subtropical climate	Continental climate
Arid or Desert climate	Alpine climate
Semiarid or Steppe climate	Subarctic climate
	Polar climate
Mediterranean climate	Climate of Antarctica
Temperate climate	

Latitude, Longitude and Altitude

Latitude gives the location of a place on earth, north or south of the equator. Longitude is almost similar but gives the location of a place on earth east or west of the equator. Altitude is the elevation of a point or object from a known level or datum.

Winds

Wind is the current of air which generally blows from hot areas to cold areas. Such winds raise the temperature of the area they are blowing over. Winds also carry moisture. The amount of precipitation a place receives also depends on the amount of moisture the winds are carrying.

High altitude areas are regions that begins 1500 meters above the sea level.

Quick Look

During the last 2 billion years, the earth's climate has alternated between an "Ice House," and a steaming "Hot House."

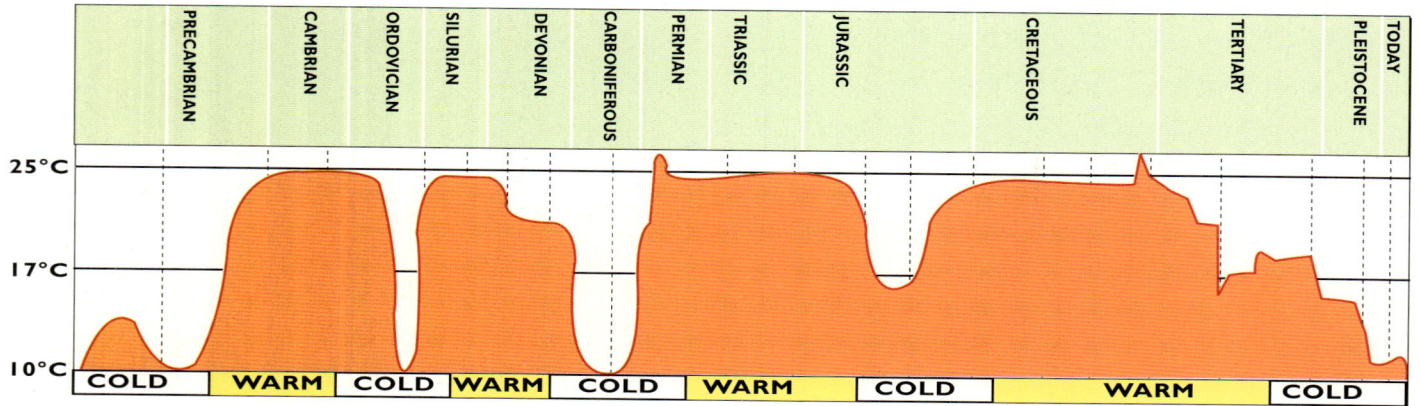

Earth's temperature timeline from Precambrian to today.

8

Distance From Sea

Places close to the sea or coastal areas have mild winters and cool summers. Places far from the sea have hot summers and cold winters.

Mediterranean Climate

The Mediterranean region is the region around the Mediterranean Sea. This region includes the southern part of Europe and the northern part of Africa. The region has cool, wet winters and hot, dry summers with little rainfall.

What is weather?

Weather is the state or condition of the atmosphere of a place over a short period. It is characterised by change in temperature, wind, atmospheric pressure, and rainfall at any given time. Most weather phenomena take place in the troposphere.

Meteorology

Meteorology is the scientific study of the atmosphere and atmospheric phenomena in relation to weather and climatic conditions. The Greek philosopher Aristotle first used the term "meteorology." In 1854, the world's first national meteorological service was established in the United Kingdom. In 1860, *The Times* published the world's first daily weather forecast.

Sea shore

Mediterranean regions have mild winters but temperatures in summer may vary depending on the region.

Weather station at Mildura Airport, Victoria, Australia.

NATURE

Flora

The earth's flora includes more than 300,000 known species of plants. Trees, herbs, bushes, shrubs, grasses, vines, ferns, mosses, and others form the earth's flora.

Rose

A rose is a perennial flowering shrub or vine. There are about 100 species of roses. They are known for their beauty and fragrance. Most rose species are native to Asia.

Orchids

The orchid family is the largest family of flowering plants. Orchids are abundant in tropical regions. All orchids have three sepals, but the flowers vary greatly in colour and shape.

Shrubs

Shrubs are low bushy plants with several stems. Shrubs provide cover and food for birds and protect the soil from erosion.

Venus Flytrap

The Venus Flytrap is a carnivorous plant that catches and digests insects and arachnids. The leaves of the Venus Flytrap are hinged and lined with stiff hair. When an insect touches the hair, the plant closes its trap.

The earth's flora.

There are around 30,000 known species of orchids

Wildflowers are herbaceous plants native to a given area.

Flora And Fauna

Conifers

Conifers are cone-bearing seed plants. All conifers are woody plants, and most are trees and a few are shrubs. Conifers include cedars, redwoods, cypresses, yews, kauris, firs, junipers, larches, spruces, and pines.

Fauna

The earth's fauna includes 3–30 million species of animals living worldwide. Mammals, primates, marsupials, birds, fish, insects, amphibians, reptiles, and others form the earth's fauna.

Mammals

Mammals are a class of animals that give birth to live young ones. There are approximately 5,000 species of mammals. Rodents, bats, carnivores, herbivores, ungulates, cetaceans, and primates are groups of mammals.

Birds

Birds are bipedal, vertebrate flying animals. All birds are warm-blooded and lay eggs. There are about 9,000–10,000 species of birds living on all seven continents.

> ### Quick Look
> 50 to 90 percent of the world's species live in the tropical regions.

The world's oldest trees are the 4,900 year-old bristlecone pines of desert mountains in California and Nevada.

Deer, gazelles and impalas are antelopes.

Birds lay eggs, which hatch into hatchlings and grow into adult birds.

NATURE

What are natural resources?
Natural occurring substances that are considered valuable in their relativity unmodified (natural) form. Water, air, land, forests, fish, topsoil, oil, natural gas, and minerals are examples of natural resources.

Oil
Oil is a black liquid obtained from deep inside the earth. Oil forms from marine organisms buried under several layers of soil, over millions of years, under extreme heat and pressure, the buried remains decompose and change into oil.

World's top five crude oil-producing countries	
1. Saudi Arabia	4. Iran
2. Russia	5. China
3. United States	

Natural Gas
Natural gas is a gaseous fossil fuel. Like oil, natural gas too was formed from the remains of ancient animals and plants. Methane (CH_4) and inert gases are the main components of natural gas.

Coal
Coal is formed from the remains of ancient plants. It is first deposited as peat, which is partially carbonised vegetable matter saturated with water. Over the time, the peat under heat and pressure changes physically and chemically into black or brownish-black rock known as coal.

An oil rig dwells oil and other petroleum products.

Photovoltaic array contains several connected solar cells, that trap sun's energy.

Coal fields are large areas used for coal deposition.

Quick Look
Humans use between 40 to 50 percent of the available freshwater on the earth.

Natural Resources

Forests

Forests are living natural renewable resources. (Forests cover approximately one-third of the earth's land area.) Forests provide large amounts of oxygen, essential oils, floss, fiber, fuel wood, fodder for cattle and other grazing animals. Forests are home to a large variety of plants and animals. Forests help in improving soil condition and reducing soil erosion.

Water

Water is the most precious natural resource that exists on our planet. Life cannot exist on earth without water. Freshwater sources on earth include rivers, lakes and groundwater. Along with the daily life and household uses, water is also used in power generation.

Wind turbines generate electricity from wind.

Dams hold back water and help in generating power.

Types of Natural Resources

- Renewable resources — resources that can be replaced.
- Non-renewable resources — resources that are used up and cannot be replaced.

Renewable Natural Resources

- Forests
- Fish
- Coffee
- Soil
- Wind
- Tides
- Solar radiations
- Water

Non-renewable Natural Resources

- Coal
- Petroleum
- Natural gas
- Propane
- Uranium ore

Natural Resource Industries

- Mining
- Petroleum extraction
- Fishing
- Forestry

Mines are excavated to extract ores and minerals.

13

NATURE

What is a mountain?
A mountain is a landform the rises high above its surroundings. Mountains generally have steep slopes and sharp or slightly rounded peaks or ridges.

Mount Everest
Mount Everest is the highest mountain in the world located on the Nepal-China border in the central Himalayas. It reaches to a height of 8,848 meters.

Karakoram Range
Karakoram Range is a mountain range in central Asia including the Karakoram Peak, second highest Peak after the Mount Everest. The Karakoram Peak reaches to a height of 8,611 meters. The borders of Tajikistan, China, Pakistan, Afghanistan, and India converge here.

Mauna Kea
Mauna Kea is the tallest mountain. It stands at a total height of 10,203 meters. However, it is only 4,205 meters above the sea. Mauna Kea is an inactive volcano on the island of Hawaii in the Pacific Ocean.

Mount Everest is considered the world's highest peak.

A mountain range is a series of mountains located closely together.

Types of Mountains

Types	Examples
Dome Mountains:	The Black Hills of South Dakota and the Adirondack Mountains of New York.
Fold Mountains:	The Alps, Himalayas, Appalachians, Russia's Ural Mountains and Andes in South America.
Fault-block Mountains:	The Sierra Nevada Mountains in North America and the Harz Mountains in Germany.
Volcanic Mountains:	The Cascade Range in Washington, Oregon and northern California, Mount St. Helens in North America and Mount Pinatubo in the Philippines.
Plateau Mountains:	The Catskill Mountains of New York and the Tibetan Plateau.

Mountains and Valleys

Types of Valleys

Type		Examples
River Valley	:	Black Canyon of the Gunnison National Park, USA, Napf region, Zurich Oberland, Engadin.
Hanging Valley	:	The Bridal Veil Falls in Yosemite National Park (USA).
Dry Valley	:	Devil's Dyke, Fulking, England and the Vale of the White Horse, Oxfordshire, England.
Misfit Valley	:	The valleys of the Cotswolds, England.
Rift Valley	:	Great Rift Valley of East Africa and The Rhine Valley between the Vosges Mountains and the Black Forest.

What is a valley?

A valley is a broad area of low-lying land situated between hills or mountains. Valleys often have a river flowing through it

Great Rift Valley

Great Rift Valley lies south of Ethiopia in east Africa. It stretches to a length of 6,400 km from the valley of Jordan River in southwestern Asia to the Zambezi River in Mozambique.

Death Valley

Death Valley comprises much of the Death Valley National Park. It is located in the region of Inyo County, California. Death Valley is the lowest, driest and hottest valley in the United States. It stretches to about 225 km in length and 26 km in width.

This deep and picturesque valley is Lotschental valey.

Death Valley National Park was established in 1933.

Quick Look

Edmund P. Hillary and Tenzing Norgay first climbed the highest mountain in 1953.

NATURE

 ## What are rainforests?

A rainforest is a large, very dense, forest in a hot, humid region. Rainforests receive heavy rain during most of the year.

 ## Amazon Rainforests

Amazon rainforests are the largest rainforests in the world. It has an area of about 6 million sq. km. The forest has more species of flora and fauna than any other ecosystem in the world. Many species of tree frogs are threatened because of deforestation in the Amazon rainforests.

The Amazon rainforests are located in the Amazon Basin of South America.

 ## Steppes

Steppes are dry grasslands found in all continents except Australia and Antarctica. They are dominated by short grasses usually without trees. Steppes have cold winters and warm summers. Many grazing animals, such as mice, rabbits, horses, antelopes inhabit these grasslands.

The grain belt in the northern Pampas.

 ## Pampas

Pampas are fertile grassy plains found in South America, especially in Argentina. They cover an area of 777,000 sq. km. from the Atlantic Ocean to the Andes Mountains. There are many kinds of animal and plant life in pampas. Cattails, water lilies and reeds are some of the plants found in pampas.

 ## Ozark Mountain Forests

The Ozark mountain forests are forests of central United States. The forests cover an area of about 62,000 sq. km. The Ozark mountain forests are a type of temperate broadleaf and mixed forests. The forests have different species of oak including red oak, white oak and hickory.

Forests and Grasslands

 ## Tropical Rainforests

Tropical rainforests are evergreen forests found near the equator. The tropical rainforests produce 40 percent of earth's oxygen. The forests receive rainfall of at least 2,500 millimeters annually and remain wet throughout the year. Broadleaf evergreens are the most abundant trees found in the tropical rainforests.

 ## What are grasslands?

Grasslands are large areas of flat land covered with grass. Few or no trees grow in grasslands.

 ## Temperate Grasslands

Temperate grasslands are located in the mid-latitudes dominated by grasses. They are found in areas, where summers are hot, winters cold, and rainfall is low all through the year. Temperate grasslands are also known as prairies.

 ## Boreal Forests

Boreal forests are found in a wide stretch across Eurasia and North America. The boreal forests have long, severe, dry winters, and moist, warm summers. Conifers such as larch, fir and spruce can be found in these forests because they can tolerate cold weather.

Temperate rainforests at Multnomah Falls, Oregon, United States.

Temperate grasslands are composed of a rich mix of grasses and have the world's most fertile soils.

A winter forest covered with snow.

Quick Look

Savanna is the other name for tropical grasslands found in areas with relatively high temperatures and seasonal rainfall. Tropical grasslands remain green throughout the wet season and change to golden-brown in the dry seasons.

NATURE

What are oceans?

Oceans are large and vast water bodies. Oceans comprise 97% of the total earth's water. There are five oceans in the world, namely, Arctic, Pacific, Atlantic, Indian and Southern Oceans. All oceans are home to a large number of plant and animal species.

Indian Ocean.

Arctic Ocean

Total area: 14.056 million sq. km.

Coastline: 45,389 km.

Description: the smallest and shallowest of all oceans.

Natural resources: sand and gravel aggregates, placer deposits, oil and gas fields, fish, marine mammals (seals and whales).

Location and border: almost completely surrounded by Eurasia and North America.

Indian Ocean

Total area: 73.6 million sq. km.

Coastline: 66,526 km.

Description: the third largest of all oceans and covers about 20% of the water on the earth's surface.

Natural resources: oil and gas fields, fish, shrimp, sand and gravel aggregates, placer deposits, polymetallic nodules.

Location and border: bounded on the north by Asia; on the west by Africa; on the east by Indochina, the Sunda Islands, and Australia; and on the south by the Southern Ocean.

Atlantic Ocean

Total area: 82.217 million sq. km.

Coastline: 111,866 km.

Description: the second largest ocean.

Natural resources: oil and gas fields, fish, marine mammals (seals and whales), sand and gravel aggregates, placer deposits, polymetallic nodules, precious stones.

Location and border: connected in the north to the Arctic Ocean, to the Pacific Ocean in the southwest, the Indian Ocean in the southeast, and the Southern Ocean in the south.

Atlantic Ocean as seen from the eastern coast of North America.

Oceans And Seas

Pacific Ocean

Total area: 165.384 million sq. km.

Coastline: 135,663 km.

Description: the largest ocean.

Natural resources: oil and gas fields, polymetallic nodules, sand and gravel aggregates, placer deposits, fish.

Location and border: lies between North and South America on the east, Asia and Australia on the west and Antarctica on the south.

Southern Ocean

Total area: 20.327 million sq. km.

Coastline: 17,968 km.

Description: the fourth largest ocean.

Natural resources: giant oil and gas fields on the continental margin, manganese nodules, sand and gravel, fresh water as icebergs; squid, whales, and seals – none exploited; krill, fish.

Location and border: the northern boundary merges into the Atlantic, Indian and Pacific Oceans.

Arabian Sea

Arabian Sea stretches to a length of 3,100 km east-west and 2,000 km north-south. Lying between the Indian and Arabian peninsulas, it is a broad arm of Indian Ocean. Indus River is the only major river that empties into it.

Quick Look

The word Mediterranean comes from the Latin language meaning "middle of the world."

Mediterranean Sea

Mediterranean Sea lies between Europe, Africa and southwestern Asia. The Strait of Gibraltar connects the Mediterranean Sea with the Atlantic Ocean and the Suez Canal, and the Gulf of Suez connects it with Red Sea. Mediterranean Sea covers an area of 2,500,000 sq.km.

Karachi beach on Arabian Sea.

The rich and diverse ecosystem of the Red Sea has more than 1,100 species of fish.

NATURE

 ## What is a river?

A river is fresh water flowing across the surface of the land, usually to the sea. It flows in a channel. The bottom of the channel is called the bed and the sides of the channel are called the banks.

 ## Nile River

Nile River is the world's longest river. The river originates in Burundi and flows north through Uganda, Sudan, and Egypt to the Mediterranean Sea. It is about 6,678 km long. The Nile River gets its name from the Greek word *Neilos*, which means a valley or river valley. The Blue Nile and the White Nile are two main tributaries of the Nile River.

 ## Mississippi River

Mississippi river is the fourth longest river in the world. It is about 3,779 km long and its basin covers an area of 3,199,999.9 sq. km. The Mississippi river flows through Montana, North Dakota, South Dakota, Nebraska, Kansas, Illinois, Alabama, Louisiana, Missouri, and Minnesota.

 ## Yangtze River

Yangtze River is the longest river in Asia and China. It is about 6,300 km long and flows through China's Sichuan Province. The main tributaries of the Yangtze river are the Han, Yalong, Jialing, Min, and Tuo He, on the north and the Wu at Zhenjiang on the south.

The Nile River passes through the capital city of Egypt, Cairo.

Map of Mississippi River.

Yangtze River is also known as Yangtse River, Yangzi River, and Yangtze Kiang.

 ## Amazon River

Amazon River is the largest and second longest river in the world. The river stretches more than 6,473 km and starts from the Andes Mountain in Peru and falls into the Atlantic Ocean. Amazon River has the largest number of tributaries than any other river.

Rivers and Lakes

What is a lake?

A lake is a water-filled depression in the crust of the earth. Most lakes are fresh water.

Lake Superior

Lake Superior is the world's largest freshwater lake. It is about 563 km long and about 257 km wide. The lake lies across the border between United States and Canada. Lake Superior is also the largest of the five Great Lakes. It contains as much water that could fill all the other Great Lakes and three other lakes.

Lake Baikal

Baikal Lake is the deepest lake in the world. It has a depth of about 1,637 meters. It is about 635 km long and about 78 km wide. The lake is situated in south-east Siberia, Russia. Baikal Lake is known as "Galapagos of Russia," because its age and isolation produced one of the richest and most unusual freshwater faunas.

Caspian Sea

Caspian Sea is the largest inland water body in the world. The lake has an area of about 371,000 sq. km. It has a mean depth of about 170 meters. The Caspian Sea is located in the northern Iran. The Caspian Sea has vast deposits of oil and natural gas.

Lake Superior receives water from about 200 rivers.

Lake Baikal has over 20 percent of the world's total unfrozen freshwater reserve.

Niagara River in Ontario, Canada.

Quick Look

Deltas are triangular areas of very fertile land formed by the rivers. The flow of a river slows down at the mouth and deposits sediments forming a delta.

NATURE

 What is a cave?
A cave is a natural underground void large enough for a human to enter.

 What is a canyon?
A canyon is a deep valley with very steep sides – often carved by a river.

 Lechuguilla Caves
The Lechuguilla Caves are located in Carlsbad Caverns National Park, New Mexico. They are the fifth longest caves reaching to a length of 193 km. Lechuguilla is also the deepest cave in the United States with a depth of 497 meters.

 Grand Canyon
The Grand Canyon is one of the most famous canyons of the world. This steep-sided gorge lies in Arizona, United States. It is more than 1,500 meters deep and only 29 km wide. A large portion of Grand Canyon is within the Grand Canyon National Park.

 Copper Canyon System
The Copper Canyon System is a group of canyons located in the Sierra Tarahumara in the southwestern part of Chihuahua in Mexico. The canyon system consists of six different canyons and has deeper portions than the Grand Canyon.

 Cotahuasi Canyon
The Cotahuasi Canyon is the deepest canyon in the world with a depth of 3,501 meters. The Cotahuasi River runs through the canyon in the Andes Mountain Range in southern Peru.

Mammoth Caves are the longest cave system in the world.

Colourado River flows through Grand Canyon.

Black Canyon is located in the Gunnison National Park, United States.

Kings Canyon is a part of Watarrka National Park in Northern Territory, Australia.

Caves And Canyons

Fish River Canyon
The Fish River Canyon in Namibia is the second largest canyon in the world after the Grand Canyon. The canyon is famous for its magnificent and incredible vastness. It is thought to be built about 500 million years ago.

Waitamo Caves
The Waitamo Caves are located on the North Island of New Zealand. They are rich with stalactites and stalagmites that form splendid mythic figures. The Glow-Worm Cave is the most popular cave of Waitamo because of an underground firmament created by glowworms.

Lava Bed Caves
The lava bed caves of northern California are famous caves. They are famous because there are many rock formations created by ancient volcanoes and earthquakes.

Quick Look
Voronja, or "Crow's Cave" is the deepest cave in the world that is located in the western Caucasus Mountains of the Georgian Republic. The depth of the cave has been verified to be 2,140 meters.

Fish River Canyon is about 160 km long and almost 550 meters deep.

Top 10 Longest Caves

Caves	Country	Area	Depth (m)
Mammoth Cave System	U.S.A.	Kentucky	563,270
Optimisticeskaja -Gypsum Cave	Ukraine	Ukrainskaja	191,500
Jewel Cave	U.S.A.	South Dakota	189,597
Holloch	Switzerland	Schwyz	165,500
Lechuguilla Cave	U.S.A.	New Mexico	154,883
Fisher Ridge Cave System	U.S.A.	Kentucky	135,990
Siebenhengste-hohgant Hohlensystem -Muttee Cave	Switzerland	Bern	135,000
Wind Cave	U.S.A.	South Dakota	131,033
Ozernaja	Ukraine	Ukrainskaja	111,000
Gua Air jernih-Lubang Batau Padeng -Cleawater Cave	Malaysia	Sarawak	109,000

NATURE

What are deserts?
A barren or desolate, especially a dry, often sandy region of little rainfall, extreme temperature and sparse vegetation.

Arabian Desert
Arabian Desert is the third largest desert in the world. It covers an area of 222,740 sq. km. The desert is located between the Red Sea and Persian Gulf. Gazelles, sand cats, oryx and spiny-tailed lizards are some of the animals that are found in Arabian Desert.

Australian Desert
Australian Desert is a group of small deserts including Great Victoria, Great Sandy, Tanami, Simpson, and Gibson. The desert spreads across the Australian continent. The deserts together cover an area of 2,299,999.98 sq. km.

Sahara Desert
Sahara Desert is the largest desert in the world. It is located on the continent of Africa. The Sahara Desert is spread in an area of 899,999.9 sq. km. It is about 5629.4 km long, from the Atlantic Ocean to the Red Sea. The desert covers almost the whole of Egypt and ten other countries including Algeria, Chad, Morocco and Libya.

Negev Desert is a rocky desert located in Israel.

Sand dunes in Death Valley, California.

Satellite image of Sahara Desert.

Namib Desert is a desert in Namibia and southwest Angola.

Deserts

Atacama Desert
The Atacama Desert covers an area of about 363, 000 sq. km. It lies in northern Chile and Peru and is bordered by the Pacific Ocean in the west and Andes Mountains in the east. It is one of the driest regions in the world. The Atacama Desert consists of sand, gravel and beds of salt.

Gobi Desert
The Gobi Desert is one of the largest deserts that stretches through China and parts of Mongolia. The desert covers an area of over 1,610 km from southwest to northeast and 800 km from north to south. The Italian traveler Marco Polo and his father and uncle were the first Europeans to travel the Gobi desert. They crossed the region in 1275.

Thar Desert
Thar Desert is located in north-western India and eastern Pakistan. It is about 805 km long and about 485 km wide. It is a sandy desert bounded by Sutlej River on the north-west, Aravalli on the east, Rann of Kachh on the south and by the Indus River plain on the west. It receives an annual rainfall averaging from 12.7 to 25.4 cm.

Takla Makan
Takla Makan is one of the largest sandy deserts in the world. It is located in the middle of the largest Basin, Tarim in Xinjiang Province, China. Takla Makan covers an area of over 33, 700 sq. km. It is also known as "the Sea of Death."

Kelso Dunes, also known as the Kelso Dune Field, is the largest field of eolian sand deposits in the Mojave Desert.

Great sand dunes in National Park, Colourado.

The Silou Desert is a desert in the south-west of Bolivia.

Quick Look
Oasis is a fertile area within a desert. An oasis always has one or more springs. It is formed when a pool of water is trapped between two rocks under the desert floor.

NATURE

 ### Geyser
The natural fountains that can shoot boiling water and steam hundreds of feet in the sky in violent eruptions.

 ### Hot Spring
A natural resource of producing warm water to the earth's surface to form a small pond.

 ### Morning Glory Pool
The Morning Glory Pool is a hot spring in Yellowstone National Park, Wyoming, United States. The spring resembles a morning glory flower and was named in 1880. The Morning Glory Pool has different colours that are caused by bacteria.

 ### Geysir
The Geysir is one of the oldest known geysers in the world located in the South West of Iceland. All the hot springs of the world are named after the Great Geysir. Geysir erupts at irregular intervals and ejects boiling water up to 60 meters in the air.

 ### Oldest Geyser
Castle Geyser is the world's oldest geyser. It is estimated by geologists that the geyser may be 5,000 and 40,000 years old. It is located in Yellowstone National Park, Wyoming, United States. Castle Geyser is still an active geyser and erupts every 10 to 12 hours. It erupts to a height of 27 meters and lasts about 20 minutes.

Castle Geyser has the largest cone of any geyser.

The Morning Glory Pool was cleaned in 1930 and over 60 dollars in pennies and other coins, tax tokens, foreign money, logs, rocks, and sticks were found from the pool.

 ### Steamboat Geyser
The Steamboat Geyser is the tallest active geyser in the world. It is located at the Norris Basin. It can erupt to more than 91 meter but more commonly, Steamboat Geyser has small eruptions and ejects water in frequent bursts of 3 to 12 meters. It thunders with powerful jets of stream.

Geysers And Hot Springs

> **Quick Look**
> Geyserite is a white or greyish silica-based deposit often found around geysers and hot springs.

Manley Hot Springs

Manley Hot Springs in Alaska has a cold, continental climate. The hot springs were discovered by a mining prospector, John in 1902. He started a vegetable farm on 278 acres of land. In 1957, the name of the hot springs was changed to the Manley Hot Springs.

Radium Hot Springs

The Radium Hot Springs are located within the boundaries of Kootenay National Park, Canada. The springs have clear, odorless and sulfurless water that was first used for medicinal and healing purposes by the Kutenai Indians. The hot springs are equipped with two pools: one heated and the other cooler for more athletic swimming.

Fountain Geyser erupts every 6.5 to 8.5 hours and has duration of about 30 minutes.

Sequence of an exploding hot spring

1. Steam rises from heated water

2. Pulses of water swell upward

3. Surface tension is broken

4. Ejected water spouts upward and falls back

27

NATURE

What is a waterfall?

Flowing water in the form of a stream over rocks which forms a sudden break in elevation.

Angel Falls

Angel Falls is the highest uninterrupted waterfalls in the world. It is 979 meters high and has an uninterrupted drop of 807 meters. It falls from the Auyantepui Mountain. The Angel Falls is in Venezuela, on the Rio Churun. The height of the falls is so great that before getting anywhere near the ground the water is vapourised by strong winds and turned into mist.

Tugela Falls

Tugela Falls is the world's second highest falls. The total height of the Tugela Falls is 948 meters and its single tallest drop is 411 meters. Tugela Falls consists of five separate free-leaping falls. The falls is located in the Kwazulu Natal region of South Africa.

Iguaçu/Iguazu/Iguassu Waterfalls

Iguassu Waterfalls is one of the largest waterfalls. It is located on the border between Argentina and Brazil on Iguassu River. The Iguassu Waterfalls ranges between 60 and 80 meters high. The falls were first discovered by a European, Álvar Núñez Cabeza de Vaca, in 1541.

The Angel Falls was discovered by an American pilot, Jimmy Angel.

Yosemite Falls in Yosemite National Park is the highest waterfall in North America.

Iguaçu Falls consists of about 275 separate waterfalls, which fall from as high as 81 meters into the gorge below.

Quick Look

Churchill Falls in Canada was known as Grand Falls. The falls was renamed after the British Prime Minister, Sir Winston Churchill in 1965.

Waterfalls

Victoria Falls

Victoria Falls on the Zambezi River located between the countries of Zambia and Zimbabwe. It is the largest waterfall in the world. Victoria Falls is 1.6 km wide and the distance from its top to the base of the gorge ranges from 61 and 128 meters. Victoria Waterfalls was named by David Livingstone after the former English Queen Victoria.

Mosi-oa-Tunya ("smoke that thunders") is the name given to Victoria Falls by local people.

Niagara Falls

Niagara Falls is located in North America on the Niagara River. The Niagara River is on the border between the United States and Canada. The Niagara Falls is a set of three waterfalls: the American Falls, the Canadian or Horseshoe Falls and the Bridal Veil Falls. In winters, the falling river and mist create ice mounds of about 15 meters thickness along the banks of falls and river.

Niagara Falls was formed about 12,000 years ago.

Yumbilla Falls

Yumbilla Falls is the fifth tallest falls in the world. The falls is a tiered fall with a height of 895 meters and has four distinct drops. Yumbilla Falls is situated in the regions of Amazonas in Peru.

Huangguoshu Waterfalls

Huangguoshu Waterfalls is the largest waterfall in Asia. It is situated in Anshun, Guizhou Province, China. It is the largest fall in China with a height of 74 meters and width of 81 meters.

Powerscourt Waterfall is 122 meters high and is located in Ireland.

29

NATURE

What is global warming?

Global warming is the increase in average temperature of earth's surface. Earth has warmed by about 0.6°C over the past 100 years. Many scientists think it has happened because of human activities. Human activities like air pollution, volcanic eruptions and solar variations are major causes of global warming.

Natural Greenhouse Effect

A layer of gases, known as the atmosphere, surrounds the earth. Some of these gases let the sun's energy escape in the space but prevent some of the heat from leaving earth's atmosphere. This keeps the earth warm enough for life to exist. These gases are called greenhouse gases, and the phenomenon is called the greenhouse effect.

Glaciers and mountain snows are rapidly melting as a result of global warming.

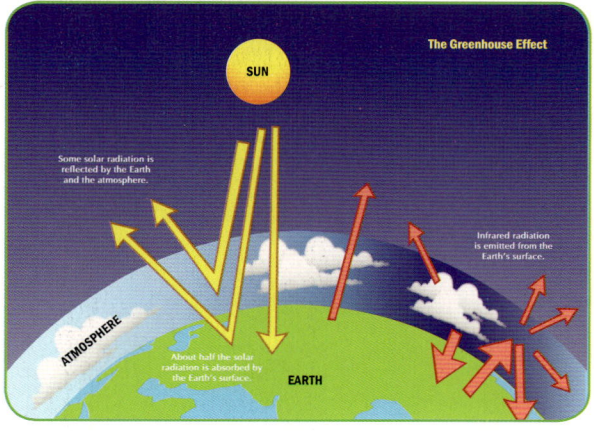
Greenhouse effect.

Facts to Know

- Global warming is more prominent over land than the oceans
- If the rate of global warming does not slow down, many species are likely to become extinct

Effects of Global Warming

- Climate change
- Frequent heat waves
- Rising sea levels
- Submerging of many islands and coastal areas
- Floods
- Droughts
- Epidemics
- Wildfires
- Change in rainfall patterns
- Scarcity of water
- Failing crops
- Drop in crop yields
- Changing weather patterns
- Declining Arctic Sea ice
- Melting of glaciers and rising of the sea level
- Animal species reduction
- Striking changes in marine animals
- Extinction of many species of plants and animals
- Outbreak of diseases

GLOBAL WARMING

Enhanced Greenhouse Effect

The enhanced greenhouse effect is the increase in the natural greenhouse effect caused by man-made activities. The enhanced greenhouse effect traps extra heat in the atmosphere that eventually causes global warming. The enhanced effect occurs at a much faster rate than the natural effect.

John Tyndall

British physicist, John Tyndall discovered that certain atmospheric gases could absorb and radiate heat. In the 1950s, Tyndall showed that water vapour, carbon di-oxide and ozone were the best absorbers of solar radiation. Tyndall was the first person to explain why the daylight sky is blue.

Quick Look

The greenhouse effect on Venus is so strong that the surface temperature can reach 482° C.

How can we reduce global warming?

- Plant more trees
- Use air conditioners only when required
- Turn off lights when not in use
- Turn off electrical and electronic appliances when not in use
- Use fluorescent light bulbs
- Use alternative fuels to run your vehicles
- Buy recyclable products
- Reduce wastes

Human Activities

Human activities that cause the enhanced greenhouse effect are:
- Burning of fossil fuels such as oil, coal and natural gas
- Clearing of forests
- Extensive rice cultivation produces methane
- Use of fertilisers
- Burning of biomass

Air pollution leads to depletion of ozone layer, a layer in earth's atmosphere that shields harmful rays from entering the earth.

Recycling is collecting and processing of used and discarded materials for reuse.

31

NATURE

Index

A
Afghanistan 2, 14
Africa 2, 4, 9-10, 15, 18-19, 24, 29
Alaska 2, 27
Algeria 2, 24
amphibians 2, 6, 11
Andes Mountains 2, 16, 24
Antarctica 2-3, 5, 8, 16, 19
Argentina 2, 16, 28
Aristotle 2, 9
Arizona 2, 22
Asia 2, 4, 10, 14-15, 18-20, 29
Atlantic Ocean 2, 16, 18-20, 24
Australia 2, 5, 16, 18-19, 22

B
bacteria 2, 7, 26
biomass 2, 31
birds 2, 6, 10, 11
Brazil 2, 28
Burundi 2, 20

C
California 2, 11, 14-15, 23-24
Canada 2, 21, 27-28
Canberra 2, 5
Chad 2, 24
Chile 2, 24
China 2, 12, 14, 20, 25, 29
Churchill, Sir Winston 2, 28

D
decaying 2, 7

E
Egypt 2, 4, 20, 24
erosion 2, 10, 13
Ethiopia 2, 15
Eurasia 2, 1-8
Europe 2, 4, 9-10, 19

F
fluorescent light bulbs 2, 31
fodder 2, 13

G
Gazelles 2, 24
Germany 2, 14
Greek 2, 8-9, 20

I
Iceland 2, 26
Indus River 2, 19, 25
Insects 2, 6
Iran 2, 12, 21

J
Jordan River 2, 15
L
Libya 2-3, 24

M
mammals 2, 6, 11, 18
marine organisms 2, 12
Methane (CH4) 2, 12
Milky Way 2
Minnesota 2
moisture 2, 8
Morocco 2, 24
Mozambique 2, 15

N
Namibia 2, 23-24
natural gas 2, 12, 21, 31
Nebraska 2, 20
New York 2, 5, 14
Norris Basin 2, 26

O
orbit 2
Oryx 2

P
Pakistan 2, 14, 25
peat 2, 12
perennial 2, 10
Peru 2, 20, 22, 24, 29
Philippines 2, 14
Polo, Marco 2, 25
power generation 2, 13
prairies 2, 17
precipitation 2, 8

Q
Queen Victoria 2, 29

R
radiate 2, 31
recyclable 2, 31
reproduction 2, 6

reptiles 2, 6, 11
River 2, 15, 19-23, 25, 28-29
Russia 2, 12, 14, 21

S
Saudi Arabia 2, 12
Siberia 2, 21
Solar radiations 2, 13
South Africa 2, 29
South Dakota 2, 14, 20, 23
spiders 2, 6
stalacities 2
stalagmites 2, 23
Strait of Gibraltar 2, 19
Sudan 2, 20

T
Tajikistan 2, 14
tree frogs 2, 16
troposphere 2, 9

U
Uganda 2, 20
United Kingdom 2, 9
United States 2, 12, 15-17, 21-22, 26
Uranium ore 2, 13

V
Venezuela 2, 28
Venus 2, 10, 31
volcanic eruptions 2, 30

Z
Zambezi 2, 15, 29
Zambia 2, 29
Zimbabwe 2, 29

32

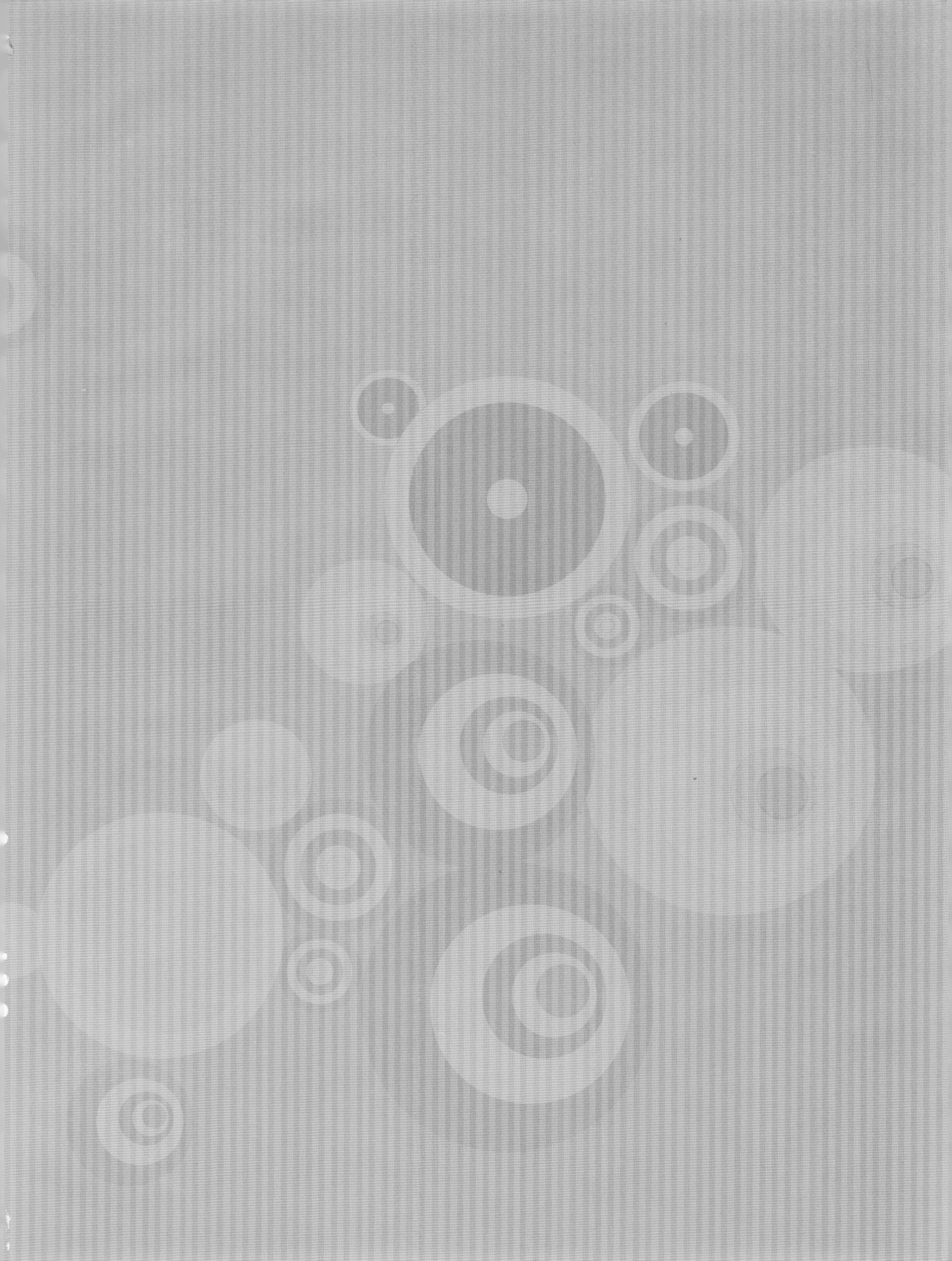